Andrew Brodie Basics

LET'S DO MENTAL MATHS

FOR AGES 9–10

with over **100** reward stickers

- Over 800 practice questions
- Regular progress tests
- Extra tips and brain booster questions

First published 2013 by Bloomsbury Publishing plc
50 Bedford Square, London, WC1B 3DP
www.bloomsbury.com

ISBN 978-1-4081-8338-0

Copyright © 2013 Bloomsbury Publishing plc
Written by Andrew Brodie
Design by Marcus Duck
Cover and inside illustrations of Digit the Dog and Andrew Brodie © Nikalas Catlow

10 9 8 7 6 5 4 3 2

A CIP record for this publication is available from the British Library.

Printed in China by Leo Paper Products

This book is produced using paper that is made from wood grown in managed, sustainable forests. It is natural, renewable and recyclable. The logging and manufacturing processes conform to the environmental regulations of the country of origin.

To see our full range of titles visit www.bloomsbury.com

BLOOMSBURY

Notes for parents

What's in this book

This is the fifth book in an exciting new series of *Andrew Brodie Basics: Let's Do Mental Maths* books. Each book contains more than 800 mental maths questions specially devised to boost children's confidence by providing plenty of practice in all the key aspects of the National Curriculum:

• Number and place value
• Addition and subtraction
• Multiplication and division
• Fractions
• Measures
• Geometry

The structure of each test follows the same pattern but the questions become gradually more difficult as the book progresses. You will notice that some questions are repeated to help your child learn and then revise vital facts such as identifying shapes: squares, triangles, rectangles and circles. Taking the time to discuss the questions with your child and helping to explain anything they find difficult will produce the best results. Answers to all the questions are provided at the back of the book.

How you can help

To begin with your child might find the tests quite tricky but as they work their way through the book and become more familiar with the different types of question their confidence will grow. At the end of every five tests there is a Progress Test which will help you and your child to review some of the key concepts and will also highlight anything they haven't understood so far. Always provide lots of encouragement and explain that they should learn from their mistakes rather than be disheartened.

Children gain confidence by learning facts that they can use in their work at school. Help your child by displaying posters on their bedroom wall, showing facts such as the times tables, days of the week and months of the year. Talk about these facts with your child and discuss the number of days in each month. You could use this rhyme to help them remember:

Thirty days has September,
April, June and November.
All the rest have thirty-one,
Except for February alone,
Which has twenty-eight days clear
And twenty-nine in each leap year.

Some children find difficulty with the concept of fractions so this is something you can help them with quite easily. Explain that the circle below is cut into eight pieces so we are dealing with eighths; seven of these are shaded so the fraction shaded is seven eighths:

Digit the Dog and Brain Boosters

Look out for useful tips from Digit the Dog who provides little snippets of mathematical information that your child needs to know or quick questions to get them thinking!

Brodie's Brain Boosters feature short mathematical problems, which can be solved by working logically. Some of these may look very straightforward but the thinking processes that your child will need to apply are important skills to practise, ready for more challenging work later. Understanding the wording of questions is a crucial aspect of problem solving so ensure that your child reads each question carefully – give some help with the vocabulary if necessary.

With lots of practice and encouragement your child will see their score improve day by day!

Score:

1 180 + 16 =

2 Add 70 to 480.

3 120 – 28 =

4 What is the difference between 900 and 170?

5 Double 32 =

6 6 x 9 =

7 What is 32 shared between 4?

8 650 ÷ 10 =

9 Write < or >. 96 ⬚ 69

10 Count in fifties: 0 50 100 150… What number comes next?

11 Round 84 to the nearest ten.

12 What is the next number in this sequence? 37, 39, 41, 43, …

13 Change this improper fraction to a mixed number $\frac{3}{2}$

14 Write this fraction as a decimal $\frac{1}{4}$

15 How many centimetres are there in 2 metres?

16 $\frac{1}{2}$ hour = ⬚ minutes

17 What is the perimeter of the rectangle?

6cm

4cm

18 1m – 63cm =

19 Write this fraction as a percentage $\frac{1}{4}$

20 What size is the missing angle?

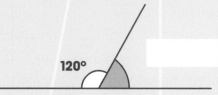

120°

Brodie's Brain Booster

I think of a number. I add 7 then multiply by 4. The answer is 48. What number did I first think of?

3

Score:

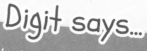
Digit says...
I think about dog biscuits a lot! I have 3 dog biscuits every day. They come in packs of 5 so 3 packs last me 5 days.

1 $240 + 31 =$

2 Add 50 to 690.

3 $110 - 47 =$

4 What is the difference between 800 and 230?

5 Double 25 =

6 $8 \times 9 =$

7 What is 24 shared between 6?

8 $720 \div 10 =$

9 Write < or >. 48   84

10 Count in fifties: 250 300 350 400...
What number comes next?

11 Round 78 to the nearest ten.

12 What is the next number in this sequence? 68, 70, 72, 74, ...

13 Change this improper fraction to a mixed number $\frac{5}{2}$

14 Write this fraction as a decimal $\frac{1}{4}$

15 How many centimetres are there in 3 metres?

16 $\frac{1}{4}$ hour =   minutes

17 What is the perimeter of the rectangle?

6cm
5cm

18 $1m - 54cm =$

19 Write this fraction as a percentage $\frac{1}{2}$

20 What size is the missing angle?

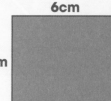
140°

TEST 3

1 350 + 43 =

2 Add 80 to 570.

3 230 – 53 =

4 What is the difference between 700 and 340?

5 Double 41 =

6 5 x 9 =

7 What is 30 shared between 5?

8 830 ÷ 10 =

9 Write < or >.   57   75

10 Count in fifties: 600 650 700 750…
What number comes next?

11 Round 62 to the nearest ten.

12 What is the next number in this sequence? 81, 83, 85, 87, …

13 Change this improper fraction to a mixed number $\frac{5}{4}$

14 Write this fraction as a decimal $\frac{1}{2}$

15 How many centimetres are there in 4 metres?

16 $\frac{3}{4}$ hour =   minutes

17 What is the perimeter of the rectangle?

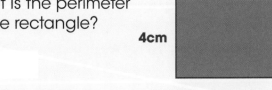
5cm
4cm

18 1m – 47cm =

19 Write this fraction as a percentage $\frac{3}{4}$

20 What size is the missing angle?

160°

Brodie's Brain Booster

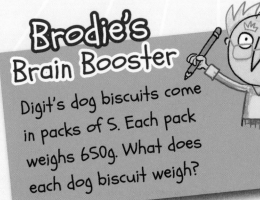

Digit's dog biscuits come in packs of 5. Each pack weighs 650g. What does each dog biscuit weigh?

5

Score:

1 630 + 59 =

2 Add 30 to 890.

3 360 − 81 =

4 What is the difference between 600 and 420?

5 Double 53 =

6 7 x 9 =

7 What is 48 shared between 6?

8 490 ÷ 10 =

9 Write < or >. 82   28

10 Count in fifties: 800 850 900 950… What number comes next?

11 Round 55 to the nearest ten.

12 What is the next number in this sequence? 65, 63, 61, 59, …

13 Change this improper fraction to a mixed number $\frac{7}{2}$

14 Write this fraction as a decimal $\frac{3}{4}$

15 How many centimetres are there in 1.5 metres?

16 $\frac{1}{2}$ hour =   minutes

17 What is the perimeter of the rectangle?

6cm

3cm

18 1m − 91cm =

19 Write this fraction as a percentage $\frac{1}{4}$

20 What size is the missing angle?

130°

Digit says…

Each pack of my dog biscuits costs £8.43. I need 3 packs for 5 days so that's more than £24. I'm worth it!

TEST 5

Score:

1 720 + 64 =

2 Add 60 to 640.

3 930 – 59 =

4 What is the difference between 800 and 290?

5 Double 24 =

6 4 x 9 =

7 What is 72 shared between 8?

8 250 ÷ 10 =

9 Write < or >. 71 ___ 17

10 Count down in fifties:
1000 950 900 850…
What number comes next?

11 Round 91 to the nearest ten.

12 What is the next number in this sequence? 88, 86, 84, 82, …

13 Change this improper fraction to a mixed number $\frac{7}{4}$

Brodie's Brain Booster

Digit needs 3 packs of dog biscuits every 5 days. Each pack costs £8.43. What is the total cost of biscuits for 5 days?

14 Write this fraction as a decimal $\frac{1}{2}$

15 How many centimetres are there in 2.5 metres?

16 $\frac{1}{4}$ hour = ___ minutes

17 What is the perimeter of the rectangle?

6cm

2cm

18 1m – 38cm =

19 Write this fraction as a percentage $\frac{1}{2}$

20 What size is the missing angle?

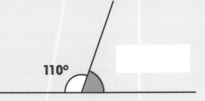

110°

Addition and subtraction

1 810 + 77 =

2 Add 40 to 770.

3 820 – 76 =

4 What is the difference between 500 and 140?

Multiplication and division

5 Double 52 =

6 11 x 9 =

7 What is 64 shared between 8?

8 970 ÷ 10 =

Number and place value

9 Write < or >. 5 [ ] 54

10 Count down in fifties:
200 150 100 50...
What number comes next?

11 Round 96 to the nearest ten.

12 What is the next number in this sequence? 93, 91, 89, 87, ...

Fractions, decimals and percentages

13 Change this improper fraction to a mixed number $\frac{9}{2}$

14 Write this fraction as a decimal $\frac{3}{4}$

15 Write this fraction as a percentage $\frac{3}{4}$

Measurement

16 What size is the missing angle?

150°

17 How many centimetres are there in 0.5 metres?

18 $\frac{3}{4}$ hour = [ ] minutes

19 What is the perimeter of the rectangle?

7cm

4cm

20 1m – 75cm =

Score chart

Test	1	2	3	4	5	Progress
Score						

Score:

1 260 + 137 =

2 Add 232 to 550

3 120 − 28 =

4 What is the difference between 1,000 and 240?

5 46 x 10 =

6 What is the product of 8 and 9?

7 56 ÷ 7 =

8 Half of 90 =

9 Write < or >. 160   610

10 Count in thirties: 0 30 60 90... What number comes next?

11 Round 479 to the nearest ten.

12 What is the next number in this sequence? 40, 43, 46, 49, …

13 Change this mixed number to an improper fraction $1\frac{1}{2}$

14 Write this decimal as a fraction: 0.5

15 2.5m =   cm

16 $\frac{1}{4}$ hour =   minutes

17 What is the perimeter of the rectangle?

4.5cm

2.5cm

18 1km − 450m =

19 Write this fraction as a percentage $\frac{1}{10}$

20 What size is the missing angle?

80°

Digit says…

I eat 3 dog biscuits every day so in April I eat 90 dog biscuits altogether. That's a big pile of dog biscuits!

TEST 7

Score:

1 410 + 245 =

2 Add 125 to 480.

3 130 – 34 =

4 What is the difference between 1,000 and 350?

5 38 x 10 =

6 What is the product of 6 and 9?

7 49 ÷ 7 =

8 Half of 70 =

9 Write < or >. 530   350

10 Count in thirties: 110 140 170 200… What number comes next?

11 Round 518 to the nearest ten.

12 What is the next number in this sequence? 52, 55, 58, 61, …

13 Change this mixed number to an improper fraction $2\frac{1}{2}$

14 Write this decimal as a fraction: 0.25

15 1.5m =   cm

16 $\frac{3}{4}$ hour =   minutes

17 What is the perimeter of the rectangle?

4.5cm

3.5cm

18 1km – 350m =

19 Write this fraction as a percentage $\frac{3}{10}$

20 What size is the missing angle?

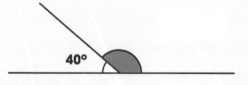

40°

Brodie's Brain Booster

Digit's dog biscuits come in packs of 5. He eats 3 dog biscuits each day. How many packs does he need for the whole of April?

Score:

1 530 + 329 =

2 Add 315 to 260.

3 150 – 56 =

4 What is the difference between 1,000 and 670?

5 93 x 10 =

6 What is the product of 7 and 9?

7 77 ÷ 7 =

8 Half of 50 =

9 Write < or >. 416   614

10 Count in thirties: 160 190 220 250...
What number comes next?

11 Round 681 to the nearest ten.

12 What is the next number in this sequence? 87, 90, 93, 96, ...

13 Change this mixed number to an improper fraction $3\frac{1}{2}$

14 Write this decimal as a fraction: 0.75

15 3.5m =   cm

16 $\frac{1}{6}$ hour =   minutes

17 What is the perimeter of the rectangle?

3.5cm

2.5cm

18 1km – 250m =

19 Write this fraction as a percentage $\frac{7}{10}$

20 What size is the missing angle?

30°

Score:

Brodie's Brain Booster

I think of a number. I multiply by 2. The answer is 70. What number did I first think of?

1 720 + 268 =

2 Add 248 to 320.

3 160 – 61 =

4 What is the difference between 1,000 and 810?

5 84 x 10 =

6 What is the product of 5 and 9?

7 42 ÷ 7 =

8 Half of 110 =

9 Write < or >. 732 _____ 327

10 Count in thirties: 610 640 670 700 … What number comes next?

11 Round 913 to the nearest ten.

12 What is the next number in this sequence? 89, 92, 95, 98, …

13 Change this mixed number to an improper fraction $4\frac{1}{2}$

14 Write this decimal as a fraction: 0.5

15 4.5m = _____ cm

16 $\frac{5}{6}$ hour = _____ minutes

17 What is the perimeter of the rectangle?

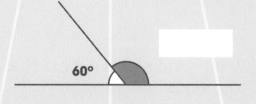

4.5cm

1.5cm

18 1km – 650m =

19 Write this fraction as a percentage $\frac{5}{10}$

20 What size is the missing angle?

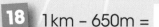

60°

Score:

1 640 + 259 =

2 Add 467 to 430.

3 170 – 75 =

4 What is the difference between 1,000 and 430?

5 27 x 10 =

6 What is the product of 4 and 9?

7 63 ÷ 7 =

8 Half of 120 =

9 Write < or >. 887   778

10 Count in thirties: 820 850 880 910…
What number comes next?

11 Round 832 to the nearest ten.

12 What is the next number in this sequence? 60, 57, 54, 51, …

13 Change this mixed number to an improper fraction $1\frac{1}{4}$

14 Write this decimal as a fraction: 0.25

15 5.5m =   cm

16 $\frac{1}{10}$ hour =   minutes

17 What is the perimeter of the rectangle?

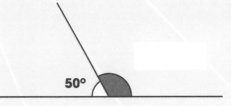

5.5cm

2.5cm

18 1km – 750m =

19 Write this fraction as a percentage $\frac{6}{10}$

20 What size is the missing angle?

50°

Digit says…

Did you know that $2\frac{1}{2}$ is called a mixed number? All I know is that $2\frac{1}{2}$ dog biscuits are better than 2 but not as good as 3.

13

Addition and subtraction

1 540 + 459 =

2 Add 135 to 740.

3 180 − 83 =

4 What is the difference between 1,000 and 590?

Multiplication and division

5 56 x 10 =

6 What is the product of 12 and 9?

7 28 ÷ 7 =

8 Half of 130 =

Number and place value

9 Write < or >. 456 ___ 654

10 Count in thirties: 890 920 950 980…
What number comes next?

11 Round 645 to the nearest ten.

12 What is the next number in this sequence? 95, 92, 89, 86, …

Fractions, decimals and percentages

13 Change this mixed number to an improper fraction $2\frac{1}{4}$

14 Write this decimal as a fraction: 0.75

15 Write this fraction as a percentage $\frac{9}{10}$

Measurement

16 What size is the missing angle?

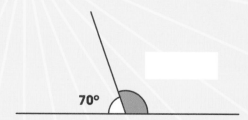

70°

17 6.5m = ___ cm

18 $\frac{1}{5}$ hour = ___ minutes

19 What is the perimeter of the rectangle?

6.5cm

2.5cm

20 1km − 850m =

Score chart

Test	6	7	8	9	10	Progress
Score						

TEST 11

1 190 + 36 =

2 2,150 plus 450 =

3 500 subtract 260 =

4 What is my change from £1 when I spend 54p?

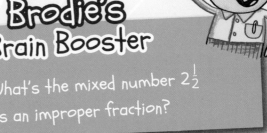

Brodie's Brain Booster

What's the mixed number $2\frac{1}{2}$ as an improper fraction?

5 6 squared =

6 8 x 7 =

7 Share 56 between 7.

8 2300 ÷ 100 =

9 Write < or >. 560   650

10 Count in forties: 0 40 80 120…
What number comes next?

11 Round 640 to the nearest hundred.

12 What is the next number in this sequence? 36, 40, 44, 48, …

13 $\frac{1}{2}$ x 6 =

14 Write $\frac{6}{10}$ as a decimal.

15 0.1m =   cm

16 $1\frac{1}{2}$ hours =   minutes

17 What is the perimeter of the rectangle?

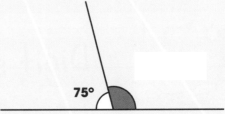

5.4cm

3.2cm

18 1l – 560ml =

19 Write this fraction as a percentage $\frac{3}{5}$

20 What size is the missing angle?

75°

15

TEST 12

1 480 + 65 =

2 3,250 plus 650 =

3 700 subtract 490 =

4 What is my change from £1 when I spend 42p?

5 4 squared =

6 12 x 7 =

7 Share 42 between 7.

8 4500 ÷ 100 =

9 Write < or >. 911 _____ 191

10 Count in forties: 30 70 110 150…
What number comes next?

11 Round 720 to the nearest hundred.

12 What is the next number in this sequence? 52, 56, 60, 64, …

13 $\frac{1}{2}$ x 8 =

14 Write $\frac{3}{10}$ as a decimal.

15 0.2m = _____ cm

16 $1\frac{1}{4}$ hours = _____ minutes

17 What is the perimeter of the rectangle?

6.1cm

3.4cm

18 1l – 240ml =

19 Write this fraction as a percentage $\frac{1}{5}$

20 What size is the missing angle?

25°

Digit says...

I am one of 8.6 million dogs in the United Kingdom. I wonder how many cats there are...

Score:

1 270 + 86 =

2 4,450 plus 250 =

3 800 subtract 540 =

4 What is my change from £1 when I spend 73p?

Brodie's Brain Booster

There are 8.6 million dogs in the United Kingdom. How many more dogs would be needed to make a total of 10 million?

5 5 squared =

6 9 x 7 =

7 Share 49 between 7.

8 6900 ÷ 100 =

9 Write < or >. 813 ____ 381

10 Count in forties: 230 270 310 350...
What number comes next?

11 Round 390 to the nearest hundred.

12 What is the next number in this sequence? 45, 49, 53, 57, ...

13 $\frac{1}{2}$ x 10 =

14 Write $\frac{4}{10}$ as a decimal.

15 0.3m = ____ cm

16 $2\frac{1}{2}$ hours = ____ minutes

17 What is the perimeter of the rectangle?

4.4cm

2.3cm

18 1l – 810ml =

19 Write this fraction as a percentage $\frac{2}{5}$

20 What size is the missing angle?

35°

17

TEST 14

Digit says...

31% of families in the United Kingdom own a dog.

1 340 + 92 =

2 6,550 plus 350 =

3 900 subtract 320 =

4 What is my change from £1 when I spend 66p?

5 7 squared =

6 4 x 7 =

7 Share 63 between 7.

8 7200 ÷ 100 =

9 Write < or >. 407   470

10 Count in forties: 470 510 550 590...
What number comes next?

11 Round 570 to the nearest hundred.

12 What is the next number in this sequence? 87, 91, 95, 99, ...

13 $\frac{1}{2}$ x 12 =

14 Write $\frac{5}{10}$ as a decimal.

15 0.4m =   cm

16 $1\frac{1}{2}$ hours =   minutes

17 What is the perimeter of the rectangle?

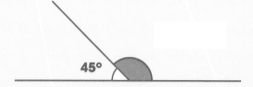

6.8cm

3.7cm

18 1l – 760ml =

19 Write this fraction as a percentage $\frac{4}{5}$

20 What size is the missing angle?

45°

Score:

1. 560 + 75 =

2. 7,150 plus 550 =

3. 600 subtract 180 =

4. What is my change from £1 when I spend 82p?

5. 8 squared =

6. 6 x 7 =

7. Share 84 between 7.

8. 8400 ÷ 100 =

9. Write < or >. 902   920

10. Count in forties: 600 640 680 720...
What number comes next?

11. Round 750 to the nearest hundred.

12. What is the next number in this sequence? 81, 77, 73, 69, ...

13. $\frac{1}{2}$ x 14 =

14. Write $\frac{7}{10}$ as a decimal.

15. 0.7m =   cm

16. $1\frac{1}{4}$ hours =   minutes

17. What is the perimeter of the rectangle?

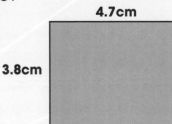

4.7cm

3.8cm

18. 1l – 690ml =

19. Write this fraction as a percentage $\frac{3}{5}$

20. What size is the missing angle?

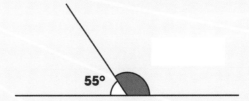

55°

Brodie's Brain Booster

31% of families in the United Kingdom own a dog. What percentage don't own a dog?

Addition and subtraction

1 640 + 61 =

2 2,150 plus 250 =

3 400 subtract 250 =

4 What is my change from £1 when I spend 27p?

Multiplication and division

5 9 squared =

6 7 x 7 =

7 Share 35 between 7.

8 5700 ÷ 100 =

Number and place value

9 Write < or >. 550   505

10 Count in forties: 790 830 870 910…
What number comes next?

11 Round 930 to the nearest hundred.

12 What is the next number in this sequence? 43, 39, 35, 31, …

Fractions, decimals and percentages

13 $\frac{1}{2}$ x 16 =

14 Write $\frac{9}{10}$ as a decimal.

15 Write this fraction as a percentage $\frac{2}{5}$

Measurement

16 What size is the missing angle?

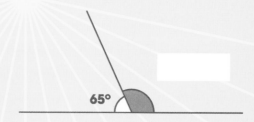

65°

17 0.8m =   cm

18 $1\frac{3}{4}$ hours =   minutes

19 What is the perimeter of the rectangle?

4.8cm

3.6cm

20 1l – 250ml =

Score chart

Test	11	12	13	14	15	Progress
Score						

Score:

1 What is the total of 680 and 230?

2 274 + 150 =

3 Decrease 820 by 350.

4 750 take away 190 =

5 Double 85 =

6 53 x 100 =

7 47 ÷ 10 =

8 What is the remainder when 25 is divided by 7?

9 Write < or >. 135   315

10 Count in eighties: 0 80 160 240…
What number comes next?

11 Round 567 to the nearest hundred.

12 What is the next number in this sequence? 29, 34, 39, 44, …

13 $\frac{1}{2}$ x 5 =

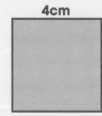

Digit says…

26% of families in the United Kingdom own a cat. I wonder why?

14 Write $\frac{42}{100}$ as a decimal.

15 0.25m =   cm

16 How many days are there in 3 weeks?

17 What is the perimeter of the square?

4cm

18 1m =   mm

19 46% of the children in a school are boys. What percentage are girls?

20 What size is the missing angle?

125°

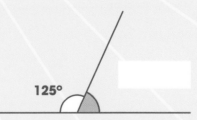

1 What is the total of 750 and 160?

2 369 + 170 =

3 Decrease 710 by 240.

4 810 take away 160 =

5 Double 65 =

6 49 x 100 =

7 38 ÷ 10 =

8 What is the remainder when 50 is divided by 7?

9 Write < or >. 724 ____ 427

10 Count in eighties: 200 280 360 440 … What number comes next?

11 Round 312 to the nearest hundred.

12 What is the next number in this sequence? 41, 46, 51, 56, …

13 $\frac{1}{2}$ x 7 =

Brodie's Brain Booster

26% of families in the United Kingdom own a cat. What percentage don't own a cat?

14 Write $\frac{69}{100}$ as a decimal.

15 0.5m = ____ cm

16 How many days are there in 4 weeks?

17 What is the perimeter of the square?

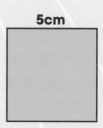

5cm

18 0.5m = ____ mm

19 31% of the children in a choir are boys. What percentage are girls?

20 What size is the missing angle?

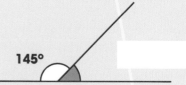

145°

Score:

1 What is the total of 590 and 350?

2 475 + 140 =

3 Decrease 930 by 460.

4 620 take away 170 =

5 Double 45 =

6 91 x 100 =

7 85 ÷ 10 =

8 What is the remainder when 60 is divided by 7?

9 Write < or >. 697 [ ] 769

10 Count in eighties: 310 390 470 550… What number comes next?

11 Round 1614 to the nearest hundred.

12 What is the next number in this sequence? 82, 87, 92, 97, …

13 $\frac{1}{2}$ x 3 =

14 Write $\frac{23}{100}$ as a decimal.

15 0.75m = [ ] cm

16 How many days are there in 5 weeks?

17 What is the perimeter of the square?

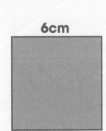

6cm

18 0.1m = [ ] mm

19 62% of the children in a rugby club are boys. What percentage are girls?

20 What size is the missing angle?

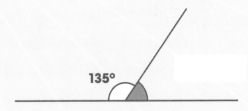

135°

Digit says...

I am lucky because I have quite a big garden to run round in. It has an area of 120 square metres.

23

1 What is the total of 470 and 280?

2 586 + 160 =

3 Decrease 520 by 260.

4 530 take away 150 =

5 Double 55 =

6 100 x 100 =

7 64 ÷ 10 =

8 What is the remainder when 40 is divided by 7?

9 Write < or >. 543   453

10 Count in eighties: 620 700 780 860… What number comes next?

11 Round 2,398 to the nearest hundred.

12 What is the next number in this sequence? 76, 81, 86, 91, …

13 $\frac{1}{2}$ x 9 =

14 Write $\frac{35}{100}$ as a decimal.

15 0.15m =   cm

16 How many days are there in 6 weeks?

17 What is the perimeter of the square?

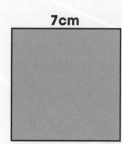

7cm

18 0.7m =   mm

19 51% of the children in an athletics club are boys. What percentage are girls?

20 What size is the missing angle?

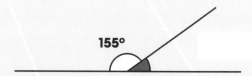

155°

Brodie's Brain Booster

What is the area of a rectangular garden that is 16m long and 8m wide?

24

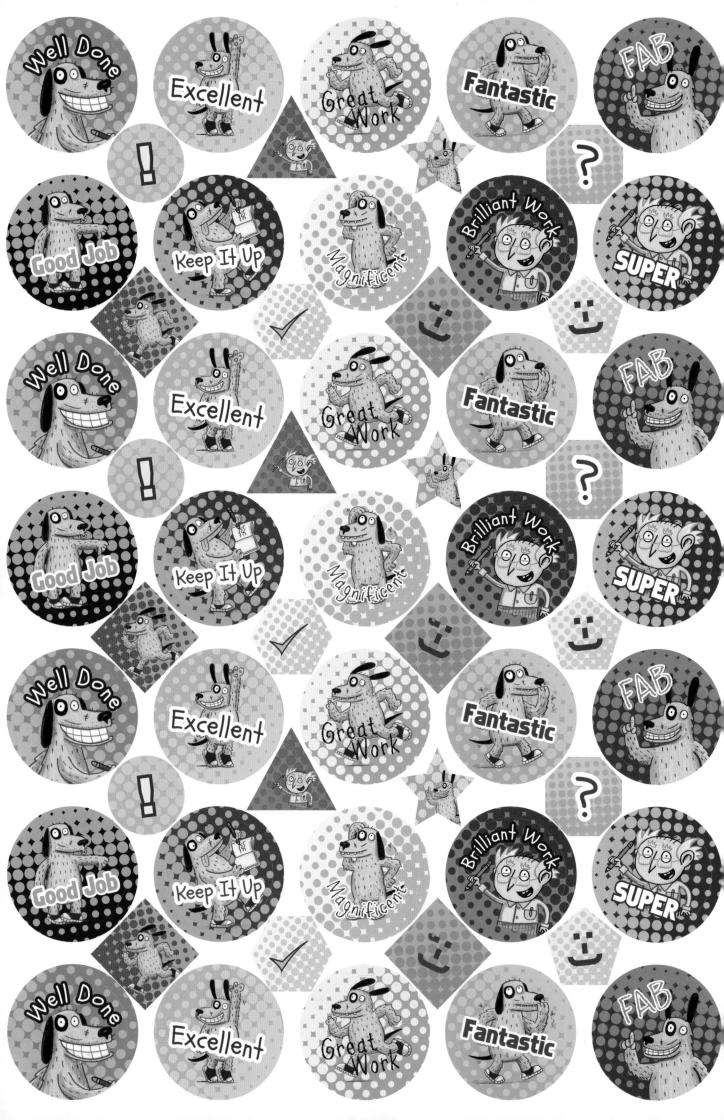

TEST 20

1 What is the total of 260 and 250?

2 687 + 130 =

3 Decrease 630 by 180.

4 830 take away 180 =

5 Double 75 =

6 82 x 100 =

7 55 ÷ 10 =

8 What is the remainder when 80 is divided by 7?

9 Write < or >. 648 ___ 846

10 Count in eighties: 730 810 890 970… What number comes next?

11 Round 8,248 to the nearest hundred.

12 What is the next number in this sequence? 119, 114, 109, 104, …

13 $\frac{1}{2}$ x 11 =

Digit says...

I eat a bowl of dog food at 5pm. That's 17.00 on a 24-hour clock.

14 Write $\frac{51}{100}$ as a decimal.

15 0.65m = ___ cm

16 How many days are there in 7 weeks?

17 What is the perimeter of the square?

3cm

18 0.4m = ___ mm

19 42% of the children in a gymnastics club are boys. What percentage are girls?

20 What size is the missing angle?

115°

25

Addition and subtraction

1 What is the total of 360 and 180?

2 431 + 170 =

3 Decrease 820 by 570

4 920 take away 140 =

Multiplication and division

5 Double 95 =

6 67 x 100 =

7 72 ÷ 10 =

8 What is the remainder when 30 is divided by 7?

Number and place value

9 Write < or >. 998 ___ 989

10 Count in eighties: 680 760 840 920… What number comes next?

11 Round 6,579 to the nearest hundred.

12 What is the next number in this sequence? 217, 212, 207, 202, …

Fractions, decimals and percentages

13 $\frac{1}{2}$ x 13 =

14 Write $\frac{75}{100}$ as a decimal.

15 39% of the children in a trampoline club are boys. What percentage are girls?

Measurement

16 What size is the missing angle?

165°

17 0.95m = ___ cm

18 How many days are there in 8 weeks?

19 What is the perimeter of the square?

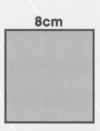

8cm

20 0.9m = ___ mm

1   3,500 + 1,300 = _____

2   I think of a number. I add 12 then subtract 7. The answer is 15. What number did I first think of?

_____

3   Add 600 to 3,800. _____

4   650 minus 470 = _____

5   The square of 7 = _____

6   Which of these numbers is a factor of 48? 7 8 9 10

_____

7   240 ÷ 3 = _____

8   Half of 600 = _____

9   Write < or >. 1,248 _____ 2,481

10   Count in sixties: 0 60 120 180… What number comes next?

_____

11   Round 3,600 to the nearest thousand.

_____

12   What is the next number in this sequence? 32, 38, 44, 50, …

_____

13 $\frac{1}{4} \times 8 =$ _____

14   Write 0.69 as a fraction. _____

15   0.1km = _____ m

16   How many hours are there in two days?

_____

17   What is the perimeter of the square?

_____

2.5cm

18   1kg – 245g = _____

19   Write this fraction as a percentage $\frac{7}{20}$

_____

20   What size is the missing angle?

_____

85°

Brodie's Brain Booster

Digit starts his evening walk at 17.45 and gets back home at 18.38. For how many minutes is he walking?

1 4,200 + 1,500 =

2 I think of a number. I add 13 then subtract 7. The answer is 8. What number did I first think of?

Digit says...

My human usually goes to bed at about 22.30. That's 10.30pm on the 12-hour clock.

3 Add 400 to 1,700.

4 850 minus 380 =

5 The square of 2 =

6 Which of these numbers is a factor of 52? 4 9 7 11

7 210 ÷ 3 =

8 Half of 800 =

9 Write < or >. 3,647   3,476

10 Count in sixties: 50 110 170 230... What number comes next?

11 Round 4,200 to the nearest thousand.

12 What is the next number in this sequence? 41, 47, 53, 59, ...

13 $\frac{1}{4}$ x 12 =

14 Write 0.73 as a fraction.

15 0.2km =   m

16 How many hours are there in three days?

17 What is the perimeter of the square?

3.5cm

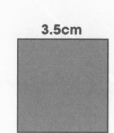

18 1kg – 316g =

19 Write this fraction as a percentage $\frac{9}{20}$

20 What size is the missing angle?

15°

1 5,100 + 1,800 =

2 I think of a number. I add 16 then subtract 4. The answer is 21. What number did I first think of?

3 Add 500 to 6,900.

4 750 minus 560 =

5 The square of 3 =

6 Which of these numbers is a factor of 65? 2 4 6 5

7 180 ÷ 3 =

8 Half of 400 =

9 Write < or >. 8,932   9,382

10 Count in sixties: 70 130 190 250… What number comes next?

11 Round 5,100 to the nearest thousand.

12 What is the next number in this sequence? 116, 122, 128, 134, …

13 $\frac{1}{4}$ × 4 =

14 Write 0.81 as a fraction.

15 0.3km =   m

16 How many hours are there in four days?

17 What is the perimeter of the square?

4.5cm

18 1kg – 750g =

19 Write this fraction as a percentage $\frac{11}{20}$

20 What size is the missing angle?

45°

Brodie's Brain Booster

I go to sleep at about 11pm and wake up again at 6.15am. For how long am I asleep?

Digit says...

I kindly wake my human at about 6.15am. That's 06.15 on the 24-hour clock.

1 6,200 + 1,400 =

2 I think of a number. I add 18 then subtract 5. The answer is 22. What number did I first think of?

3 Add 700 to 8,500.

4 550 minus 270 =

5 The square of 8 =

6 Which of these numbers is a factor of 72? 7 9 11 13

7 270 ÷ 3 =

8 Half of 500 =

9 Write < or >. 6,555   5,666

10 Count in sixties: 460 520 580 640... What number comes next?

11 Round 6,800 to the nearest thousand.

12 What is the next number in this sequence? 327, 333, 339, 345, ...

13 $\frac{1}{4}$ x 16 =

14 Write 0.97 as a fraction.

15 0.4km =   m

16 How many hours are there in five days?

17 What is the perimeter of the square?

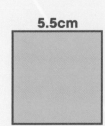

5.5cm

18 1kg – 460g =

19 Write this fraction as a percentage $\frac{13}{20}$

20 What size is the missing angle?

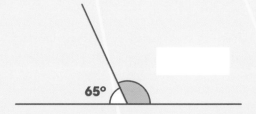

65°

Score:

1   2,700 + 1,300 =

2   I think of a number. I add 24 then subtract 7. The answer is 19. What number did I first think of?

3   Add 800 to 9,200.

4   950 minus 160 =

5   The square of 9 =

6   Which of these numbers is a factor of 24? 7 8 9 10

7   360 ÷ 3 =

8   Half of 700 =

9   Write < or >. 7,308 _____ 8,730

10   Count in sixties: 590 650 710 770… What number comes next?

11   Round 8,400 to the nearest thousand.

12   What is the next number in this sequence? 424, 418, 412, 406, …

13 $\frac{1}{4}$ x 24 =

14   Write 0.29 as a fraction.

15   0.5km = _____ m

16   How many hours are there in six days?

17   What is the perimeter of the square?

6.5cm

18   1kg – 595g =

19   Write this fraction as a percentage $\frac{17}{20}$

20   What size is the missing angle?

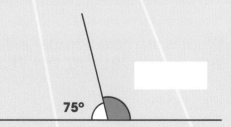

75°

Brodie's Brain Booster

Digit had a long walk of about 12.4km yesterday. How many metres are equal to 12.4km?

Addition and subtraction

1 5,100 + 1,900 =

2 I think of a number. I add 17 then subtract 8. The answer is 25. What number did I first think of?

3 Add 900 to 7,500.

4 450 minus 170 =

Multiplication and division

5 The square of 6 =

6 Which of these numbers is a factor of 30? 6 7 8 9

7 150 ÷ 3 =

8 Half of 900 =

Number and place value

9 Write < or >. 4,747 ⬚ 7,474

10 Count in sixties: 820 880 940 1,000… What number comes next?

11 Round 7,500 to the nearest thousand.

12 What is the next number in this sequence? 721, 715, 709, 703, …

Fractions, decimals and percentages

13 $\frac{1}{4}$ × 20 =

14 Write 0.43 as a fraction.

15 Write this fraction as a percentage $\frac{19}{20}$

Measurement

16 What size is the missing angle?

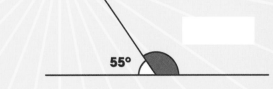

55°

17 0.6km = ⬚ m

18 How many hours are there in seven days?

19 What is the perimeter of the square?

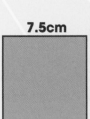

7.5cm

20 1kg – 827g =

Score chart

Test	21	22	23	24	25	Progress
Score						

TEST 26

Score:

Digit says...

My lead is extendable. Usually I keep my human quite close with the lead at about 1.4m.

1   4,600 + 2,700 =

2   I think of a number. I subtract 12 then add 8. The answer is 30. What number did I first think of?

3   3,850 plus 450 =

4   What is the difference between 1,400 and 320?

5   Which of these numbers is a prime number? 8 9 10 11

6   12 x 2 = 16 +

7   I think of a number. I multiply by 6 and divide by 2. The answer is 12. What number did I think of?

8   240 ÷ 30 =

9   Write < or >. 68,000   86,000

10   Count in seventies: 0 70 140 210... What number comes next?

11   Round 2,381 to the nearest thousand.

12   What is the next number in this sequence? 34, 41, 48, 55, ...

13 $\frac{1}{4}$ of £1 =

14   1 – 0.6 =

15   0.2l =   ml

16   How many minutes are there in two hours?

17   What is the perimeter of the square?

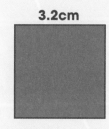

3.2cm

18   A square has perimeter of 20cm. How long is each side?

19   Write this fraction as a percentage $\frac{13}{20}$

20   What size is the missing angle?

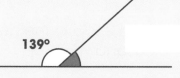

139°

33

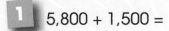

Convert 1.4m to centimetres.
Now convert it to millimetres.

1 5,800 + 1,500 =

2 I think of a number. I subtract 16 then add 7. The answer is 40. What number did I first think of?

3 4,750 plus 350 =

4 What is the difference between 1,700 and 560?

5 Which of these numbers is a prime number? 12 13 14 15

6 14 x 2 = 13 +

7 I think of a number. I multiply by 9 and divide by 2. The answer is 27. What number did I first think of?

8 180 ÷ 30 =

9 Write < or >. 93,000   39,000

10 Count in seventies: 90 160 230 300… What number comes next?

11 Round 2,975 to the nearest thousand.

12 What is the next number in this sequence? 29, 36, 43, 50, …

13 $\frac{1}{4}$ of £2=

14 1 – 0.7 =

15 0.4l =   ml

16 How many minutes are there in three hours?

17 What is the perimeter of the square?

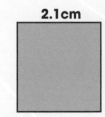

2.1cm

18 A square has perimeter of 24cm. How long is each side?

19 Write this fraction as a percentage $\frac{23}{50}$

20 What size is the missing angle?

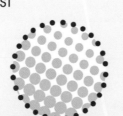

127°

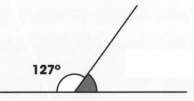

TEST 28

Score:

1   6,400 + 3,800 =

2   I think of a number. I subtract 14 then add 8. The answer is 60. What number did I think of?

3   6,250 plus 950 =

4   What is the difference between 1,500 and 240?

5   Which of these numbers is a prime number? 15 16 17 18

6   15 x 2 = 12 +

7   I think of a number. I multiply by 7 and divide by 2. The answer is 21. What number did I first think of?

8   270 ÷ 30 =

9   Write < or >. 57,000   75,000

10   Count in seventies: 180 250 320 390… What number comes next?

11   Round 5,264 to the nearest thousand.

12   What is the next number in this sequence? 75, 82, 89, 96, …

13 $\frac{1}{4}$ of £3=

14   1 – 0.9 =

15   0.9l =   ml

16   How many minutes are there in four hours?

17   What is the perimeter of the square?

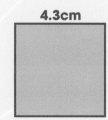
4.3cm

18   A square has perimeter of 32cm. How long is each side?

19   Write this fraction as a percentage $\frac{33}{50}$

20   What size is the missing angle?

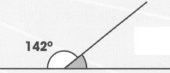
142°

Digit says...

Sometimes I let my human get to the very end of my lead, which is 7.2m long.

Score:

1 7,500 + 1,900 =

2 I think of a number. I subtract 13 then add 9. The answer is 50. What number did I first think of?

3 5,450 plus 850 =

4 What is the difference between 1,600 and 180?

5 Which of these numbers is a prime number? 21 22 23 24

6 16 x 2 = 20 +

7 I think of a number. I multiply by 5 and divide by 2. The answer is 30. What number did I first think of?

8 360 ÷ 30 =

9 Write < or >. 18,000   81,000

10 Count in seventies: 510 580 650 720... What number comes next?

11 Round 8,699 to the nearest thousand.

12 What is the next number in this sequence? 221, 214, 207, 200, ...

13 $\frac{1}{4}$ of £5=

14 1 – 0.4 =

15 0.7l =   ml

16 How many minutes are there in ten hours

17 What is the perimeter of the square?

5.2cm

18 A square has perimeter of 40cm. How long is each side?

19 Write this fraction as a percentage $\frac{43}{50}$

20 What size is the missing angle?

154°

Brodie's Brain Booster

What's 7.2m in centimetres? Now convert it to millimetres.

TEST 30

Score: [ ]

1 5,700 + 2,600 = [ ]

2 I think of a number. I subtract 17 then add 6. The answer is 70. What number did I first think of?

[ ]

3 1,850 plus 550 = [ ]

4 What is the difference between 1,800 and 440?

[ ]

5 Which of these numbers is a prime number? 27 28 29 30

[ ]

6 13 x 2 = 18 + [ ]

7 I think of a number. I multiply by 3 and divide by 2. The answer is 45. What number did I think of?

[ ]

8 210 ÷ 30 = [ ]

9 Write < or >. 98,000 [ ] 89,000

10 Count in seventies: 640 710 780 850... What number comes next?

[ ]

11 Round 9,111 to the nearest thousand.

[ ]

12 What is the next number in this sequence? 100, 93, 86, 79, ...

[ ]

13 $\frac{1}{4}$ of £9= [ ]

14 1 – 0.5 = [ ]

15 0.6l = [ ] ml

16 How many minutes are there in twenty hours?

[ ]

17 What is the perimeter of the square?

[ ]

5.3cm

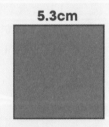

18 A square has perimeter of 16cm. How long is each side?

[ ]

19 Write this fraction as a percentage $\frac{17}{50}$

[ ]

20 What size is the missing angle?

[ ]

126°

37

Addition and subtraction

1 3,700 + 2,700 =

2 I think of a number. I subtract 18 then add 5. The answer is 40. What number did I first think of?

3 2,650 plus 750 =

4 What is the difference between 1,900 and 550?

Multiplication and division

5 Which of these numbers is a prime number? 31 32 33 34

6 17 x 2 = 25 +

7 I think of a number. I multiply by 11 and divide by 2. The answer is 44. What number did I first think of?

8 150 ÷ 30 =

Number and place value

9 Write < or >. 47,000   74,000

10 Count in seventies: 230 300 370 440… What number comes next?

11 Round 9,789 to the nearest thousand.

12 What is the next number in this sequence? 327, 320, 313, 306, …

Fractions, decimals and percentages

13 $\frac{1}{4}$ of £10 =

14 1 – 0.8 =

15 Write this fraction as a percentage $\frac{27}{50}$

Measurement

16 What size is the missing angle?

138°

17 0.8l =   ml

18 How many minutes are there in twenty-four hours?

19 What is the perimeter of the square?

3.4cm

20 A square has perimeter of 28cm. How long is each side?

Score:

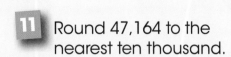

1 1,750 + 3,140 =

2 I think of a number. I add 130 then subtract 80. The answer is 70. What number did I first think of?

3 Increase 2,750 by 450.

4 What is my change from £5 when I spend 72p?

5 Which of these numbers is not a multiple of 7? 42 56 64 70

6 20 x 4 = 160 ÷

7 I think of a number. I multiply by 30 and divide by 2. The answer is 75. What number did I first think of?

8 2400 ÷ 3 =

9 Write < or >. 158,697   97,658

10 Count in twenty-fives: 0 25 50 75... What number comes next?

11 Round 47,164 to the nearest ten thousand.

12 What is the next number in this sequence? 37, 45, 53, 61, ...

13 $\frac{1}{4}$ of 1kg=

14 1 – 0.35 =

15 0.7kg =   g

16 How many days are there in January?

17 A rectangle has perimeter of 20cm. Two sides are 6cm long. How long are the other sides?

18 What is the area of the square?

4cm

19 Write this fraction as a percentage $\frac{6}{25}$

20 What size is the missing angle?

76°

Brodie's Brain Booster

Digit's new lead cost £17.08. How much less than £20 is that?

39

1   2,350 + 4,230 =

2   I think of a number. I add 120 then subtract 40. The answer is 90. What number did I first think of?

3   Increase 3,850 by 450.

4   What is my change from £5 when I spend 98p?

5   Which of these numbers is not a multiple of 8? 40   46   48   56

6   30 x 4 = 360 ÷

7   I think of a number. I multiply by 60 and divide by 2. The answer is 120. What number did I first think of?

8   1,800 ÷ 3 =

9   Write < or >. 324,106   106,324

10   Count in twenty-fives: 80   105   130   155... What number comes next?

11   Round 53,692 to the nearest ten thousand.

12   What is the next number in this sequence? 42, 50, 58, 66, ...

13 $\frac{1}{4}$ of 2kg=

14   1 – 0.48 =

15   0.1kg =   g

16   How many days are there in March?

17   A rectangle has perimeter of 20cm. Two sides are 7cm long. How long are the other sides?

18   What is the area of the square?

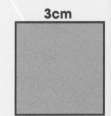

3cm

19   Write this fraction as a percentage $\frac{4}{25}$

20   What size is the missing angle?

54°

TEST 33

Score:

1 4,160 + 1,720 =

2 I think of a number. I add 110 then subtract 50. The answer is 80. What number did I first think of?

3 Increase 1,650 by 450.

4 What is my change from £5 when I spend 54p?

5 Which of these numbers is not a multiple of 9? 37 45 54 63

6 10 x 4 = 160 ÷

7 I think of a number. I multiply by 40 and divide by 2. The answer is 160. What number did I first think of?

8 1,200 ÷ 3 =

9 Write < or >. 907,544 ___ 97,544

10 Count in twenty-fives: 275 300 325 350… What number comes next?

11 Round 75,449 to the nearest ten thousand.

12 What is the next number in this sequence? 113, 121, 129, 137, …

13 $\frac{1}{4}$ of 3kg=

14 1 – 0.92 =

15 0.4kg = ___ g

16 How many days are there in April?

17 A rectangle has perimeter of 24cm. Two sides are 8cm long. How long are the other sides?

18 What is the area of the square?

6cm

19 Write this fraction as a percentage $\frac{9}{25}$

20 What size is the missing angle?

62°

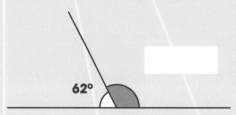

Brodie's Brain Booster

Digit's new collar cost £10.49 and the cat's collar cost £2.25. What's the difference in cost?

41

1 5,630 + 2,330 =

2 I think of a number. I add 140 then subtract 80. The answer is 120. What number did I first think of?

3 Increase 4,550 by 450.

4 What is my change from £5 when I spend 67p?

5 Which of these numbers is not a multiple of 6? 30 36 44 48

6 15 x 4 = 180 ÷

7 I think of a number. I multiply by 90 and divide by 2. The answer is 180. What number did I think of?

8 2,100 ÷ 3 =

9 Write < or >. 623,708   783,602

10 Count in twenty-fives: 170 195 220 245... What number comes next?

11 Round 89,870 to the nearest ten thousand.

12 What is the next number in this sequence? 207, 215, 223, 231, ...

13 $\frac{1}{4}$ of 5kg=

14 1 − 0.68 =

15 0.8kg =   g

16 How many days are there in May?

17 A rectangle has perimeter of 18cm. Two sides are 6cm long. How long are the other sides?

18 What is the area of the square?

5cm

19 Write this fraction as a percentage $\frac{7}{25}$

20 What size is the missing angle?

83°

Digit says...

My human bought my new lead for £17.08 and my new collar for £10.49, which is a total of £27.57. The cat only got a cheap collar!

Score:

1 7,420 + 2,140 =

2 I think of a number. I add 150 then subtract 90. The answer is 130. What number did I first think of?

3 Increase 6,750 by 450.

4 What is my change from £5 when I spend 85p?

5 Which of these numbers is not a multiple of 9? 80 90 180 135

6 25 x 4 = 1,000 ÷

7 I think of a number. I multiply by 50 and divide by 2. The answer is 125. What number did I first think of?

8 3,600 ÷ 3 =

9 Write < or >. 121,211   211,121

10 Count in twenty-fives: 365 390 415 440… What number comes next?

11 Round 17,023 to the nearest ten thousand.

12 What is the next number in this sequence? 775, 783, 791, 799, …

13 $\frac{1}{4}$ of 9kg=

14 1 − 0.24 =

15 0.3kg =   g

16 How many days are there in June?

17 A rectangle has perimeter of 22cm. Two sides are 8cm long. How long are the other sides?

18 What is the area of the square?

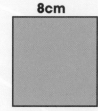

8cm

19 Write this fraction as a percentage $\frac{12}{25}$

20 What size is the missing angle?

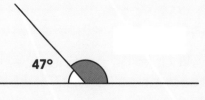

47°

Addition and subtraction

1 8,330 + 1,660 =

2 I think of a number. I add 160 then subtract 80. The answer is 130. What number did I first think of?

3 Increase 4,350 by 450.

4 What is my change from £5 when I spend 38p?

Multiplication and division

5 Which of these numbers is not a multiple of 7? 36 42 49 56

6 12 x 4 = 144 ÷

7 I think of a number. I multiply by 70 and divide by 2. The answer is 175. What number did I first think of?

8 2,700 ÷ 3 =

Number and place value

9 Write < or >. 300,009 _____ 900,003

10 Count in twenty-fives: 900 925 950 975... What number comes next?

11 Round 36,500 to the nearest ten thousand.

12 What is the next number in this sequence? 969, 977, 985, 993, ...

Fractions, decimals and percentages

13 $\frac{1}{4}$ of 10kg =

14 1 – 0.55 =

15 Write this fraction as a percentage $\frac{21}{25}$

Measurement

16 What size is the missing angle?

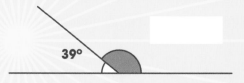

39°

17 0.6kg = _____ g

18 How many days are there in September?

19 A rectangle has perimeter of 24cm. Two sides are 7cm long. How long are the other sides?

20 What is the perimeter of the square?

7cm

ANSWERS

	Test 1	Test 2	Test 3	Test 4	Test 5	Progress Test 1
1	196	271	393	689	784	887
2	550	740	650	920	700	810
3	92	63	177	279	871	744
4	730	570	360	180	510	360
5	64	50	82	106	48	104
6	54	72	45	63	36	99
7	8	4	6	8	9	8
8	65	72	83	49	25	97
9	>	<	<	>	>	<
10	200	450	800	1000	800	0
11	80	80	60	60	90	100
12	45	76	89	57	80	85
13	$1\frac{1}{2}$	$2\frac{1}{2}$	$1\frac{1}{4}$	$3\frac{1}{2}$	$1\frac{3}{4}$	$4\frac{1}{2}$
14	0.25	0.25	0.5	0.75	0.5	0.75
15	200	300	400	150	250	75%
16	30	15	45	30	15	30°
17	20cm	22cm	18cm	18cm	16cm	50
18	37cm	46cm	53cm	9cm	62cm	45
19	25%	50%	75%	25%	50%	22cm
20	60°	40°	20°	50°	70°	25cm

	Test 6	Test 7	Test 8	Test 9	Test 10	Progress Test 2
1	397	655	859	988	899	999
2	782	605	575	568	897	875
3	92	96	94	99	95	97
4	760	650	330	190	570	410
5	460	380	930	840	270	560
6	72	54	63	45	36	108
7	8	7	11	6	9	4
8	45	35	25	55	60	65
9	<	>	<	>	>	<
10	120	230	280	730	940	1010
11	480	520	680	910	830	650
12	52	64	99	101	48	83
13	$\frac{3}{2}$	$\frac{5}{2}$	$\frac{7}{2}$	$\frac{9}{2}$	$\frac{5}{4}$	$\frac{9}{4}$
14	$\frac{1}{2}$ or $\frac{5}{10}$	$\frac{1}{4}$ or $\frac{25}{100}$	$\frac{3}{4}$ or $\frac{75}{100}$	$\frac{1}{2}$ or $\frac{5}{10}$	$\frac{1}{4}$ or $\frac{25}{100}$	$\frac{3}{4}$ or $\frac{75}{100}$
15	250	150	350	450	550	90%
16	15	45	10	50	6	110°
17	14cm	16cm	12cm	12cm	16cm	650
18	550m	650m	750m	350m	250km	12
19	10%	30%	70%	50%	60%	18cm
20	100°	140°	150°	120°	130°	150m

	Test 11	Test 12	Test 13	Test 14	Test 15	Progress Test 3
1	226	545	356	432	635	701
2	2,600	3,900	4,700	6,900	7,700	2,400
3	240	210	260	580	420	150
4	46p	58p	27p	34p	18p	73p
5	36	16	25	49	64	81
6	56	84	63	28	42	49
7	8	6	7	9	12	5
8	23	45	69	72	84	57
9	<	>	>	<	<	>
10	160	190	390	630	760	950
11	600	700	400	600	800	900
12	52	68	61	103	65	27
13	3	4	5	6	7	8
14	0.6	0.3	0.4	0.5	0.7	0.9
15	10	20	30	40	70	40%
16	90	75	150	90	75	115°
17	17.2cm	19cm	13.4cm	21cm	17cm	80
18	440ml	760ml	190ml	240ml	310ml	105
19	60%	20%	40%	80%	60%	16.8cm
20	105°	155°	145°	135°	125°	750ml

	Test 16	Test 17	Test 18	Test 19	Test 20	Progress Test 4
1	910	910	940	750	510	540
2	424	539	615	746	817	601
3	470	470	470	260	450	250
4	560	650	450	380	650	780
5	170	130	90	110	150	190
6	5,300	4,900	9,100	10,000	8,200	6,700
7	4.7	3.8	8.5	6.4	5.5	7.2
8	4	1	4	5	3	2
9	<	>	<	>	<	>
10	320	520	630	940	1,050	1,000
11	600	300	1,600	2,400	8,200	6,600
12	49	61	102	96	99	197
13	2.5	3.5	1.5	4.5	5.5	6.5
14	0.42	0.69	0.23	0.35	0.51	0.75
15	25	50	75	15	65	61%
16	21	28	35	42	49	15°
17	16cm	20cm	24cm	28cm	12cm	95
18	1000	500	100	700	400	56
19	54%	69%	38%	49%	58%	32cm
20	55°	35°	45°	25°	65°	900

	Test 21	Test 22	Test 23	Test 24	Test 25	Progress Test 5
1	4,800	5,700	6,900	7,600	4,000	7,000
2	10	2	9	9	2	16
3	4,400	2,100	7,400	9,200	10,000	8,400
4	180	470	190	280	790	280
5	49	4	9	64	81	36
6	8	4	5	9	8	6
7	80	70	60	90	120	50
8	300	400	200	250	350	450
9	<	>	<	>	<	<
10	240	290	310	700	830	1,060
11	4,000	4,000	5,000	7,000	8,000	8,000
12	56	65	140	351	400	697
13	2	3	1	4	6	5
14	$\frac{69}{100}$	$\frac{73}{100}$	$\frac{81}{100}$	$\frac{97}{100}$	$\frac{29}{100}$	$\frac{43}{100}$
15	100	200	300	400	500	95%
16	48	72	96	120	144	125°
17	10cm	14cm	18cm	22cm	26cm	600
18	755g	684g	250g	540g	405g	168
19	35%	45%	55%	65%	85%	30cm
20	95°	165°	135°	115°	105°	173g

	Test 26	Test 27	Test 28	Test 29	Test 30	Progress Test 6
1	7,300	7,300	10,200	9,400	8,300	6,400
2	34	49	66	54	81	53
3	4,300	5,100	7,200	6,300	2,400	3,400
4	1,080	1,140	1,260	1,420	1,360	1,350
5	11	13	17	23	29	31
6	8	15	18	12	8	9
7	4	6	6	12	30	8
8	8	6	9	12	7	5
9	<	>	<	<	>	<
10	280	370	460	790	920	510
11	2,000	3,000	5,000	9,000	9,000	10,000
12	62	57	103	193	72	299
13	25p	50p	75p	£1.25	£2.25	£2.50
14	0.4	0.3	0.1	0.6	0.5	0.2
15	200	400	900	700	600	54%
16	120	180	240	600	1200	42°
17	12.8cm	8.4cm	17.2cm	20.8cm	21.2cm	800
18	5cm	6cm	8cm	10cm	4cm	1440
19	26%	46%	66%	86%	34%	13.6cm
20	41°	53°	38°	26°	54°	7cm

	Test 31	Test 32	Test 33	Test 34	Test 35	Progress Test 7
1	4,890	6,580	5,880	7,960	9,560	9,990
2	20	10	20	60	70	50
3	3,200	4,300	2,100	5,000	7,200	4,800
4	£4.28	£4.02	£4.46	£4.33	£4.15	£4.62
5	64	46	37	44	80	36
6	2	3	4	3	10	3
7	5	4	8	4	5	5
8	800	600	400	700	1,200	900
9	>	>	>	<	<	<
10	100	180	375	270	465	1,000
11	50,000	50,000	80,000	90,000	17,000	40,000
12	69	74	145	239	807	1,001
13	250g	500g	750g	1.25kg	2.25kg	2.5kg
14	0.65	0.52	0.08	0.32	0.76	0.45
15	700	100	400	800	300	84%
16	31	31	30	31	30	141°
17	4cm	3cm	4cm	3cm	3cm	600
18	16cm²	9cm²	36cm²	25cm²	64cm²	30
19	24%	16%	36%	28%	48%	5cm
20	104°	126°	118°	97°	133°	49cm²

Brodie's Brain Booster

Test 1	5
Test 3	130g
Test 5	£25.29
Test 7	18
Test 9	35
Test 11	5/2
Test 13	1.4 million
Test 15	69%
Test 17	74%
Test 19	128m²
Test 21	53
Test 23	7 hours 15 minutes
Test 25	12,400
Test 27	140cm 1400mm
Test 29	720cm 7200mm
Test 31	£2.92
Test 33	£8.24
Test 35	£2.43

Digit says...

"Well done and see you next time"

48